Glimpses of Heworth, Felling & Windy Nook

by Anthea Lang

Introduction

This book follows on from Memories of Felling published in 2015. This new book not only re-visits Felling but takes a look at Heworth and Windy Nook as well. As with the previous book, it is not a chronological or a comprehensive history but tries to show how changes, some chosen, some forced, impacted on the lives of people – portrayed here through the use of postcards, photographs and advertisements.

I would like to thank everyone who has so willingly allowed me to use images – I am only sorry I have been unable to use them all.

Special thanks are due to George Nairn, Edward Jennings, Richard Jennings, Maggie Thacker, Owen Parry, Helen Hudson, Chris McGregor, Gerry McGregor, Norman Dunn, Claire Cullingworth and Beamish Museum. And of course to my publisher Andrew Clark without whose help and assistance this book would never have seen publication.

This book is dedicated to Joan Hewitt and the late Peter Hayward who both did so much to promote the history of the area.

Anthea Lang, November 2016

A troop of Heworth Boy Scouts 1908. Highburn House is in the background.

Previous page: Stuart, Thomas, Anne and Ella Sisterson with a shop assistant outside their drug store, c. 1900.

Front cover: Tram terminus, St Mary's Church, 1924.

Back cover, top: Members of St Mary's Church Choir, 1972.

Back cover, bottom: A play by Sunday School children from Windy Nook in 1931 – 'Jill and Jack the sailor, caught in a compromising situation in a scene from Queen Lily and her Subjects.'

Copyright Anthea Lang 2016
First published in 2016 by
Summerhill Books PO Box 1210, Newcastle-upon-Tyne NE99 4AH
www.summerhillbooks.co.uk   email: summerhillbooks@yahoo.co.uk
ISBN: 978-1-911385-07-3

No part of this publication may be reproduced, stored in a mechanical retrieval system, or transmitted, in any form or by any means, electronic, mechanical, photocopying, recording or otherwise, without prior permission of the author.

In the Beginning ...

Felling, Heworth and Windy Nook were all once part of the Township of Heworth, which contained the areas of Bill Quay, Nether Heworth (the area around St Mary's Church), Wardley, Follonsby, High Heworth (the village containing Heworth Colliery), Windy Nook, Carr Hill, High Felling, Low Felling and Felling Shore. The area was all part of Jarrow and remained so until 1843 when Heworth was created a separate parish.

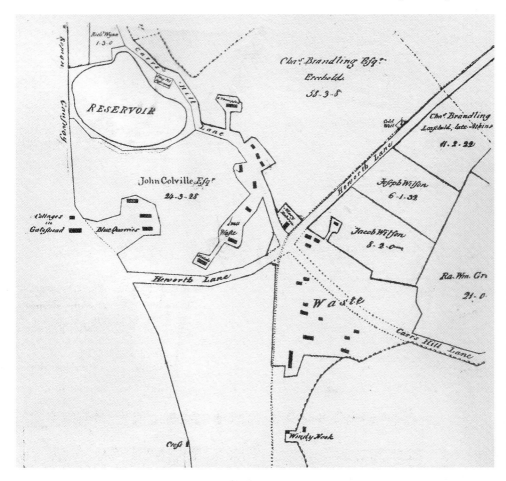

Left: An 18th century map. Heworth Common is shown here marked as waste. Heworth Lane at the right of the picture is today's Coldwell Avenue and Holly Hill

There were originally only two roads for the whole area: the High Lane (the original road to Sunderland which crossed Split Crow Lane) and Heworth Lane which followed the edge of Heworth common going up as far as Windy Nook.

The southern section of Windy Nook, High Felling and Carr Hill (an area of about 450 acres) was covered by Heworth Common and the people who lived here paid rent to the Dean and Chapter of Durham. The process of enclosing Heworth common was agreed in 1766, with two of the original petitioners to Parliament advocating enclosure, Charles Brandling (Felling Hall) and John Colville (White House) buying large portions of it when it was parcelled up and sold in lots. The area of Windy Nook wasn't included in the sale. Enclosure improved farming as fields could be hedged and land drainage installed but it caused hardship to many of the people who had previously farmed small sections of it.

The Township of Heworth was originally governed by a Select Vestry – a group of men elected at an annual Easter Vestry meeting. When John Hodgson became Perpetual Curate of Jarrow in 1808, he chose to live in Heworth rather than in Jarrow and it was with Heworth's affairs rather than Jarrow's that he and his Vestry concerned themselves. But with the coming of Matthew Plummer in 1833, a High Church man who resisted change, increased voting rights, industrialisation and an increasing population (between 1801-1851 the population had trebled from 3,000 to 9,000), the scene was ripe for conflict. The character of the Select Vestry began to change with staunch Anglicans being at least partially replaced by Non-Conformists – many of whom were the very manufacturers whose works were now changing the appearance of much of the area.

In 1866, electoral reform meant many working men were given the right to vote for the first time. In the same year, Felling Parish was created separately from Heworth, with Felling's Christ Church largely paid for by the owners of Felling Chemical Works, the Redmaynes and Pattinsons. Christ Church was Low Church – in stark contrast to the High Church services offered at St Mary's Heworth by Plummer. New housing sprang up, particularly at Felling Shore, and shops and houses were built on what became Felling High Street.

Tensions rose and in 1867, 28 men, many of them shopkeepers and local traders, infuriated by the Vestry's seeming apathy to deal with problems such as health and sanitation, signed a petition to adopt the Local Government Act. They lost the vote but the following year the Act was adopted and in 1875, boundaries were extended to include much of Windy Nook and High Felling. Felling now had its own Local Board and two years later, Matthew Plummer, aged and weary, resigned. His successor Dr James Steel was much less confrontational and accepted that change had to come. When Felling was created an Urban District Council in 1894, Heworth's importance was diminished for ever.

Left: The Heworth pinfold situated beside the Wheatsheaf and alongside Heworth Hall lodge which can be seen at the right of the photograph.

Pinfolds were features of medieval settlements and were used to house stray animals. When an animal was claimed, a fee was made which usually went to the church.

Heworth Post Office and Schools. These buildings are now only memories – they were demolished for the construction of Heworth Metro Interchange.

Heworth

Think of Heworth today and many people will immediately think of a large traffic roundabout but in earlier times Heworth had a very different appearance. This was a rural landscape, fields, pastures and streams and its name comes from heah + worth which literally means a high enclosure around a field. There were three distinct areas: Heworth Shore beside the river; Nether Heworth around St Mary's Church; and High Heworth, which became the colliery area alongside Windy Nook.

The first mention of the Manor de Heworth comes in 1133. Land delineation was as confused then as it often is today. A court case held in 1305 accused John Gategang of Gateshead of taking four acres of land at Heworth. He was found guilty and ordered to make restoration and pay damages.

Medieval residents fished at Heworth Shore, with its valleys, streams, burns and woodland but by the late 18th century, this green and pleasant land had been replaced by an industrial landscape, populated by bleach fields, potteries and colour works. It became a poor area and at Cuthbertson's brewery here on 13th January 1783 there is a record of a fat ox being killed and divided between about 50 poor people. Each received 7 pounds of beef, one 6d loaf and a gallon of beer *'to their great relief at this season, when every necessary of life is so dear.'*

When the Squires Arms public house was advertised for sale here in 1858 it was described as *'eligibly situated ... in a populous neighbourhood in immediate vicinity of chemical and other manufactories.'* This might not sound an appealing location but the inn would have done a brisk trade with the thirsty chemical workers when they came off shift.

However, the centre, Nether (or Lower) Heworth, remained an altogether more pleasant area with St Mary's Church as the building around which life largely revolved.

St Mary's Church

St Mary's Church.

St Mary's Church has always been the main building in Heworth. It was originally established as a Chapel of Ease to St Paul's Church at Jarrow until Heworth became a parish in its own right in 1843.

When the Reverend John Hodgson came to Heworth in 1808, he preached in a chapel here which had been built in 1711 but had replaced a much earlier building. Hodgson was one of the most educated clergymen in the area. He was also a notable antiquarian although he went to his grave believing that the pot and selection of Anglo Saxon coins he found at Heworth in 1812 proved that a chapel had existed here since 685AD. It was not until 1980, when plans were underway to celebrate the church's 1300th anniversary, that the coins were found to be no more than Georgian forgeries. The anniversary was never held although other deeds and documents suggest that a chapel stood on or near this site from at least the 12th century.

Hodgson wanted Heworth to be a parish in its own right but this never happened in his lifetime. However, he did at least manage to build a new church. The design is attributed to the Newcastle architect John Stokoe although it seems he was probably working to Hodgson's plans. The foundation stone of the church was laid on 23rd May 1821.

It was Hodgson's successor, Matthew Plummer, who succeeded in forming a new parish of Heworth in 1843, thus becoming its first Vicar. Plummer was also responsible for building two other churches – St Alban's at Windy Nook and Christ Church at Felling. Plummer did not have an easy time of it as the new incumbent. A section of his congregation accused him of introducing Popish practices such as psalm and prayer chanting and eventually a special church court had to be held at Heworth as a result of which Plummer was vindicated.

In 1858, St Mary's was described as *'a handsome Gothic cruciform stone structure, erected in 1822 near the site of the old church.'*

This wasn't quite grand enough however for Plummer's successor James Steel who came to Heworth in 1877 and remained until his death 40 years later. Steel wanted a much finer church.

Over the next few years new features were added to the interior. These included a new oak floor, new font (although the 18th century font was retained), new pews to replace the old Georgian box pews, a new Harrison organ, and a new pulpit and rood screen, both of which were carved in the Ralph Hedley workshops. (Ralph Hedley was a noted wood and stone carver whose work can be found throughout the North East.) A clock was added to the tower in 1883.

Interior of St Mary's showing the rood screen and new pews.

Arguably St Mary's finest stained glass is a memorial window erected to the memory of James Steel's wife. Elizabeth Steel died in 1911 and when her coffin was carried into St Mary's for the funeral service, schoolchildren carrying bunches of flowers lined either side of the churchyard path. The window, designed by the Edinburgh firm of Ballantynes, was unveiled by Lord Northbourne on 22nd May 1912.

For the first 20 years of his incumbency, Steel and his family lived in a fairly plain vicarage which was built just south of the railway line (*see page 16*). Like the church, Steel probably thought it could be improved upon so he had a new vicarage built to the east of the churchyard. This was both grander and larger with 10 rooms and was in stark contrast to the accommodation of the poor sexton who lived nearby. In 1911, he and his family – all 11 of them – were living in just two rooms!

James Steel, Vicar of Heworth from 1877-1917.

The new vicarage of 1897. This was demolished in 1975.

The original vicarage later became the Public Assistance Office before becoming one of the casualties of the Felling bypass and demolished in 1958.

James Steel died in 1917 and in his Will written shortly after his wife died, he left £200 to the Vicar and Churchwardens to be invested and the annual income distributed *'among the deserving poor who are members of the Church of England'* twice a year on the birthdays of himself and his wife.

Further improvements to the church continued to be made throughout the 20th century.

To celebrate King George V's Silver Jubilee in 1935, an oak lych-gate on a base of Heworth Burn sandstone was added to the church and formally unveiled on 17th July 1937 (by which time two changes of Kings had occurred – George V was dead, his eldest son Edward VIII had abdicated and George VI was now on the throne). The lych-gate was later moved slightly south when the Felling bypass was constructed.

The church pictured before the addition of the lych-gate.

The new lych-gate constructed by Pelaw CWS.

The new lych-gate in its original situation.

A major restoration of the church began with a campaign in 1953 to raise £10,000. The work was completed in 1959 and in the 1970s the exterior of the church underwent a complete facelift when the grime of many years was removed in a major stone cleaning operation. A new peal of bells was installed in 1986.

Members of St Mary's Choir, 1950.

St Mary's churchyard is extensive and there are a number of fine graves. It was planted by the well-established local nurseryman William Falla in 1823 – and appropriately, he is buried here. Among the many interesting graves in the churchyard is one to the miners' leader, Thomas Hepburn and a memorial service to Thomas Hepburn is held at the graveside each year.

In 1915, a military funeral held here for Private Robert Turner of Heworth who served in the 9th battalion of the Durham Light Infantry, was described at the time as one of the largest and most impressive on record with crowds lining the route and the churchyard. Turner died on 6th May 1915 following a hand injury received during the Battle of Ypres. He has a Commonwealth war grave in the south east section of the churchyard.

Right: The Commonwealth war grave to Private Robert Turner.

There are a number of other Commonwealth war graves for the dead of both world wars but there is only one to a woman. This commemorates Catherine Hedley Rogers, a member of Queen Mary's Army Auxiliary Corps who died aged 27 on 9th November 1918, just two days before Armistice was declared.

One of the saddest funerals took place in August 1902 with the burial of Mary Ina Stewart. This little girl disappeared while visiting relatives in Bill Quay. After a frantic search, her body was finally discovered inside brickworks, concealed by grass.

A cart man, Thomas Nicholson, was later hanged at Durham for her murder. The funeral cortege walked from Bill Quay to Heworth with the coffin carried on slings held by four men including her father.

The memorial carries the words:

'Erected by a sympathetic public to the memory of
MARY INA STEWART
who died August 16th 1902 aged 7 years.'

Right: St Mary's churchyard. The memorial to Mary Ina Stewart is at the front of the photograph.

St Mary's churchyard closed for burials in new graves on 1st June 1934 and a new civil cemetery, built on land adjoining opened in 1940. In the same year, part of the churchyard had to be removed in order to create a new entrance from Sunderland Road. As compensation, the church received £400 together with a small piece of land behind the war memorial.

Left: St Mary's churchyard in 2016. Many graves here are still in remarkably good condition.

Flour, Coal and Stone

In the original Heworth area, there were numerous watermills producing corn and barley including a steam powered corn mill. By 1833, 16 mills were recorded powered by either wind or water although within 10 years, over a third of these had disappeared.

The Heworth Burn powered at least four corn mills along its length. The Low Heworth mill was situated on the east bank of the Heworth Burn between High Heworth Lane and the foot of what is today The Drive. It ground corn and oatmeal, was built of stone and rubble with a pantile roof and had a water wheel approximately 15 feet in diameter. The earliest mention of this mill comes when it was assessed for rates of £15 in 1763. The former mill house was later occupied by Norman Alexander, a monumental mason.

Another mill – the Heworth Dene Forge mill may have stood on the site of an earlier common forge used for the medieval village. The Hind family were the last to run this forge and they produced a variety of good quality spades and shovels – often used by the many miners of the district. When the mill closed, the Hind family took over the Low Heworth mill and used it as a shovel forge.

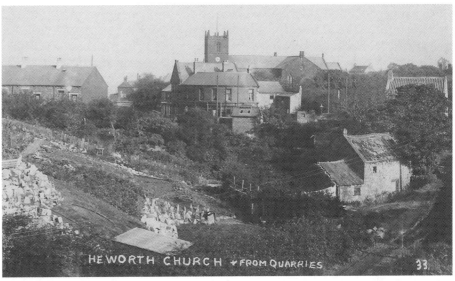

St Mary's Church and the Swan Inn as viewed from the quarries at the turn of the 20th century. The rear view of Low Heworth watermill (*shown below*) can be seen at the right. The photograph also shows the derelict foot road into Tate Brown's Low Burn quarry (*see page 10*).

Low Heworth mill, c. 1870.

The High Lane corn mill.

It is difficult today to imagine there were ever watermills at Heworth but here is the proof. When frozen over, they must have looked spectacular as in the image above on the right.

There was another mill at High Heworth known as the High Lane mill which stood above Boiston's quarry.

By the end of the 19th century, these mills had ceased working and the only evidence remaining that there were watermills here today is the old Mill House standing at the bottom of The Drive and the street name Watermill Lane.

Heworth was noted for its quarries with twelve separate quarries being listed in the Heworth Chapelry rates book for 1807. Stone was plentiful in the area – the Heworth Band is a name given to a sweep of carboniferous sandstone lying above and between the coal measures covering the Heworth parish. John Hodgson, Heworth's Curate, was the son of a

Cumbrian stone mason and when he first came to Heworth, lodged with the Kell family, who by then were building their business and owned various quarries. Richard Kell and Co, became the largest quarry firm in the area. It wasn't long before John Hodgson and Jane Bridget Kell (Richard's daughter) were married and when Richard Kell died in 1823, he left his quarries to his young grandson Richard Wellington Hodgson who later became Mayor of Gateshead. R.W. Hodgson took over the Windy Nook Grindstone quarries (*see page 42*) and also owned the Leam Head and Battery quarries. Not surprisingly, the Kell quarries provided the stone used to build John Hodgson's new church at Heworth.

Quarries came in all shapes and sizes – some big, some small, some were short lived while others, like Tate Brown, which became the last working quarry, lasted well into the 20th century. The quarries were at their busiest between 1830 to 1900 producing good quality stone for many notable buildings. To the south of High Lane was the High Burn quarry of Boiston and Clark while Heworth Low Burn quarry was owned by Adam Tate and William Brown. There were four colours of stone in the Heworth Band; white, grey, brown and blue of which blue was the hardest and best quality stone.

Heworth Low Burn quarry.

The Tate Brown quarries lay between High Lane and High Heworth Lane reached by the footpath shown on previous page. Tate Brown's supplied stone to many of the local chemical works and other industrial companies in the area. The firm later bought the Crow Hall quarry which produced predominantly brown stone used for the Duke of Cumberland Hotel and Christ Church Institute on Sunderland Road. After Thomas Boiston died, Tate Brown's took over his High Burn quarry. In the 1920s, Tate Brown's were employing about 80 men.

Heworth Colliery

This was a very old colliery, originally owned by the Blackett family and worked since the early 18th century. By 1819, the High Main seam was worked out and it became a ventilation shaft for the new pit which opened the same year on the road to Whitehill. A whole little village, now disappeared, sprang up around the colliery.

In 1894, 1,000 men and boys were employed here producing a daily output of 1,100 tons of coal. During the 20th century, there were frequent strikes (often short-lived) as wages were cut during times of recession. In 1910, a seam closed meaning 254 men and boys lost their jobs.

Left: High Heworth Colliery and Primitive Methodist Chapel. The chapel opened in 1878. It had a face lift in 1907 when it was closed for a few weeks for a *'reformation'*. Owing to *'a goodly supply of paint and soap and water, the church has now a bright and cheerful appearance.'*

The 1920s were particularly hard times in the area even though 1921 seems to have been a boom year for the colliery as it was employing over 2,000 men. However, when the coal export market collapsed in 1925, the coal owners wanted the men to work longer hours for less money. A General Strike was the result which lasted nationally for two weeks. Durham miners however, continued their strike until November 1926.

Soup Kitchen outside the Primitive Methodist Chapel in 1912.

Men who wanted to accept the terms and work weren't popular. The Times reported on 7th September 1926: *'Exciting scenes were witnessed at the Fanny Pit, Gateshead owned by Heworth Coal Company this afternoon, when 50 men, who had started in the morning were leaving work. The men had descended the pit unmolested at 6 o'clock in the morning on the agreed terms of an 8 hour day and a 10% reduction in wages. A crowd began to collect at the pit head in the morning and by 2 o'clock, when the men came up from their work, it had grown to over 2,000. Three miners who tried to get away were caught by the crowd and severely handled. A small number of police were present but were unable to cope with the crowd. A woman was knocked down and had a leg broken. Some of the miners ran for a tram car, but the vehicle was surrounded and 6 windows were broken by stones. The women in the crowd were more infuriated than the men and kicked and clawed at the miners. Mr John English the agent for the colliery was knocked to the ground and several attempts were made to kick him. Police reinforcements were rushed to the scene and the crowd dispersed.'*

The Fanny Pit, Heworth Colliery.

Heworth Colliery Relief Committee, 1926.

As so many families were affected by severe hardship because of the strike, Felling's education authority established 10 canteens throughout the district to provide breakfast and dinners for children. Miners families could apply for relief but the miners themselves couldn't and so soup kitchens were set up to help them. This wasn't the first time these had made an appearance however as they were introduced in an earlier strike in 1912 (*see picture above*).

The situation had hardly improved when a further drop in wages was demanded in 1928.

After arbitration, miners were forced to comply but as the selling price of coal continued to fall, short time working was introduced and by 1935, employment was only half what it had been in 1921. Foot wear funds were set up and in 1933, 6,000 adults in the parish signed a petition for extra winter relief. The pit was partially closed in 1940 although it was hoped to carry on land sale trade.

During the Second World War, the colliery had the dubious distinction of being the location of the first death of a Bevin Boy (young men conscripted into the collieries instead of the armed forces). Robert Henry Hale of Islington, London came to Heworth Colliery to work as a shaft lad. Only a month after he had completed his training on 4th May 1944, he was struck by a cage and fatally injured.

In 1935, Heworth Colliery welfare hall and ground was opened with six tennis courts, plus bowling and putting greens. The building contained a main hall for dances and a small terrace which could be used for tea. One of the people who helped arrange the finance for this was Peter Lee, the trade unionist and miners' leader, whose name would eventually be given to a County Durham 'new town'.

In 1870, the colliery established its own school for the children of colliery workers. However, this didn't long survive the opening of the new board school at Windy Nook and it later became St Cuthbert's Mission for St Mary's Church until closing in the 1950s.

Temporary closure of Heworth Colliery, 1940.

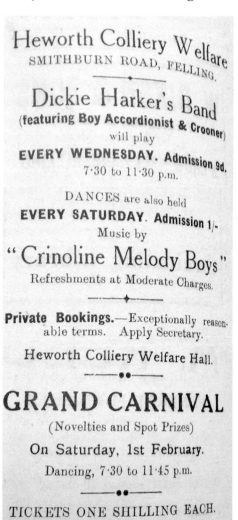

Events held at the welfare hall in 1935.

Wilson Rockett (1884-1931) in his invalid cart outside Heworth Colliery. Wilson had been a hewer at the colliery but was injured underground and had to have both legs amputated. His fellow miners had a collection and bought this cart for him.

The colliery had its own cricket team and football team as well as a prize silver band. In 1906, the band won the championship of the Northumberland and Durham Brass Bands Association. In 1935, they broadcast on the region's 5NO radio station. They were frequently asked to play at miners' funerals.

Top right: Heworth Colliery cricket team, 1921.

Right: Heworth Colliery football team, 1910.

The colliery closed in June 1963. Although there was never a major disaster here, approximately 115 miners lost their lives during the life of the colliery, the last in 1957.

Farming

Employment was also to be had on the local farms. These had been a feature in Heworth since medieval times. They were often leased from the wealthy merchants who had bought land to build their mansions and were usually quite small – 100 acres or less. They were used as grazing land for sheep and cattle and for growing rotation cops such as barley, turnips, potatoes etc.

John Russell (1742-1832), the Heworth squire who lived at Heworth Hall, had three tenanted farms on his estate (which wasn't covered by the Enclosure Award). These were Low Heworth, Nether Heworth Farm and Heworth Grange. Heworth Grange was reputedly a medieval monastery farm and was situated at the triangle formed by the present day High Heworth Lane, High Lanes and Sunderland Road Villas. Heworth Cemetery now covers part of the farmland.

Low Heworth Farm house was situated on the west side of the Low Lane and the squire farmed the land between Low Lane and Stoneygate lane.

Nether Heworth Farm stood opposite Heworth Hall and its fields stretched eastwards towards Bill Quay. When Nether Heworth Hall was demolished by its owner, the builder William Knott, in 1932, it was described as the oldest house in Heworth. Knott then built Nether House on the site.

Another farm was situated at High Heworth, sandwiched between quarries and coal pits. For a time it was occupied by the Rev John Hodgson although he never farmed the land preferring instead to cultivate his vegetable garden and write his 'History of Northumberland'. It was later lived in by the Adamson family of Windy Nook prior to the new Windy Nook vicarage being built. For the rest of the 19th century, it was occupied by a variety of farmers, who rented from the owners – the Wylam family who were 'gentlemen farmers'.

Whitehill Farm, Heworth Colliery.

Trains, Trams and Trouble!

Heworth's position at a crossroads has unfortunately meant that the area has always been affected by changes in types of transport and in improvements to traffic flow and junctions. This has been happening since the end of the 18th century when the new turnpike road, today's Sunderland Road, was built in 1796. Heworth contains a number of streams (usually referred to as burns) which are now mostly hidden. One of these, the Heworth Burn, once ran in front of the Swan Inn and was originally crossed by a low bridge. When Sunderland Road was constructed, this hollow had to be artificially raised. It had to be raised again in 1883 for the introduction of steam trams. At this point, the burn was culverted and the bridge demolished.

The seal of the Brandling Junction Railway Company.

The Brandlings, the major coal owning family from Felling, began operating an early passenger rail service in 1839 under the name of the Brandling Junction Railway. The first train to run on their Gateshead to Monkwearmouth route however wasn't a passenger train but a coal train of 61 wagons filled with coal from one of Lord Ravensworth's collieries en-route to Wearmouth docks. The railway directors travelled with the train and were given an *'elegant cold collation with champagne and other wines in profusion'*, courtesy of Sir Hedworth Williamson (a local politician).

Ordinary passengers on the railway weren't so well served however. The Brandling's trains were uncomfortable and the stations were draughty and cramped. Often people had to travel in the same carriages as animals and it wasn't long before George Hudson (the 'railway king') had bought the Brandlings out and the railway became part of his Newcastle and Darlington Railway in 1845.

The line from Newcastle to South Shields was finally electrified on 14th March 1938 – 34 years after electrification was introduced on the north side of the river.

Trams were another new form of transport. In 1883 the Gateshead Tramways Company opened three lines – the third of which ran from Gateshead High Street to Felling and terminated beside the Swan Inn (a Heworth landmark since at least the mid 1800s). These were steam hauled and by the 1890s, were running at a 20 minute frequency.

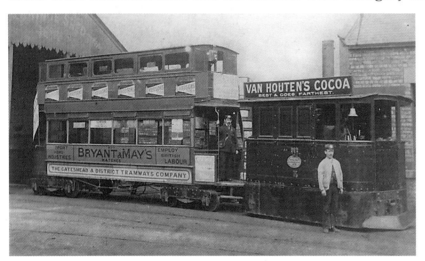

A Heworth steam tram. The engine advertises Van Houtens cocoa while the passenger car carries an advert for Bryant and May matches.

Heworth Village looking east with a tram at its terminus outside the Swan Inn in 1905. St Mary's Terrace is at the right.

Animals as well as people were carried but many people were unhappy that whilst they had to pay for their babies and children, dogs could travel free. The fare from Heworth to Sunderland Road end (where the trams refuelled) cost 1d. The last steam tram ran on 8th May 1901 and the following day, residents saw their first electric trams operating.

14

The Gateshead Tramway Company later tried to extend their tram service but were refused permission so the tramway company began operating a motor bus service between Heworth and High Jarrow in 1913. This complemented an existing bus service which ran from Heworth to Washington and began operating the same year. Golfers at the newly founded Heworth Golf Club at Jingling Gate no doubt appreciated the new motor buses – when the club began it was said that travelling to the course meant *'necessitating a brisk walk from the Heworth car terminus.'*

In 1923, once tramlines had been installed on the High Level Bridge, the tram service was extended to Newcastle. This proved hugely popular – the fare was 3d which included the halfpenny bridge toll.

When The Drive was constructed in 1924, the tram terminus had to be moved to make way for it and a new wider road laid which passed in front of the school. It is hard to imagine today that opposite the church and on the site of the present Metro Interchange in a hollow were once six little wooden cottages. These had to be demolished so that road widening could take place and their site was filled in. The level of the village centre was now artificially raised and consequently the village lost much of its character.

Accidents involving trams weren't uncommon. In 1933 the side of a tramcar was ripped off by a lorry overtaking a horse and cart which resulted in the death of a female tram passenger and provoked this response in the local newspaper: *'It does not appear safe now-a-days to be an ordinary passenger on a tramcar.'*

Heworth tram terminus, c. 1910. Heworth Council School in the background, the Swan Inn is at the right.

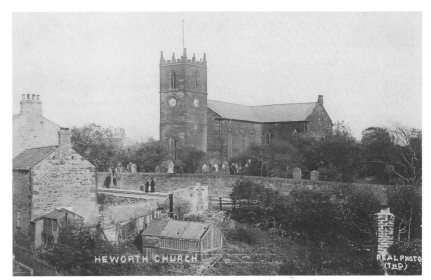

St Mary's Church with cottages.

Tram terminus, St Mary's Church, 1924. The tram's destination is shown as the Monument at Newcastle while the motor bus proclaims Monkton, Jarrow and Gateshead on its destination board.

But even in the 1930s, it seemed the day of the tram was over. When a roundabout was first proposed for Heworth in 1936, it was thought likely that *'the tramways would probably be abandoned within the next few years.'*

During the Second World War, the trams had to keep to an eight mile an hour limit. An anti-tank barrier was placed across Sunderland Road which meant that trams were unable to turn the corner and so the terminus had to be moved again – this time to Ridley Terrace on Sunderland Road.

Right: A Heworth tram at the terminus in Heworth village in 1947. In the background on the left are the gables of Heworth School with the waiting room and toilets in front. The last tram to operate on the route was the number 34 which made its final journey on Sunday, 5th March 1951 when it left the Haymarket, Newcastle for Heworth at 10.55pm.

As traffic increased, coupled with numerous traffic accidents, it was obvious that improvements had to be made. Street lamps were added to the road leading from Heworth to Wardley in 1907 and Belisha beacons, 'Slow', 'Halt' and 'Cross Road' signs were added in 1936. These were followed by zebra crossings in the early 1950s.

But all these were small scale measures. From the 1930s onwards, there had been calls to create a new road which would bypass Felling. Huge disruption to Heworth was caused by the construction of this bypass (which didn't actually bypass Felling but cut through the middle of it) and its associated roundabout. Stretching for 3.2 miles, the bypass cost £2.5 million and took nearly two and a half years to build. The main contractor was Wimpey's and part of the cost was given by the Ministry of Transport. It finally opened in 1959 and was heralded as a major traffic improvement although it decimated Heworth in the process. The railway bridge at Heworth was demolished as was the parish hall, the Constitutional Club and part of the grounds of Heworth Hall.

A portion of consecrated ground had to be removed to make way for the bypass in 1959 and a plaque was erected to show the location.

Heworth village. The wall of St Mary's Church on the right of the photograph and the Constitutional Club (the original vicarage) on the left. The Belisha beacon dates this photograph to the mid 1930s.

Left: The section of road leading to Wardley and White Mare Pool during the course of construction of the bypass. The church lych-gate and tower can be seen in the background with the school on the right.

The final large scale traffic disruption to Heworth came in 1975 with the construction of Heworth Metro Interchange, with the main contractor being the firm of Balfour Beatty. Construction involved the demolition of the school, school house, clinic, Ward's shop, toilets and waiting room.

For a number of years, after opening in 1981, Heworth was the southern terminus of the Metro line.

Right: How Heworth looked before the Metro system. Looking from Sunderland Road to St Mary's Church in the 1960s. Part of Heworth Infant & Junior School (the Council school) can be seen to the left – this is now the site of Heworth Metro station.

Education and Health

Heworth's first school was provided by the Rev John Hodgson, who firmly believed that education could improve the lives of the labouring poor. He opened the school on 18th June 1815 – a day which would go down in history as the Battle of Waterloo. The school was largely paid for by the Heworth villagers and cost around £250. It was built on the south side of today's Heworth Drive and was over two floors with a 'live in' school master who also did double duty as the Parish Clerk. The school was so popular that it soon became too small so in 1835, a new house was built for the schoolmaster and the upper floor of the school was then used for girls classrooms.

Heworth Council School shown in 1905 viewed from the south.

Once the Education Act came into force in 1870 (making education compulsory for 5-11 year olds) there weren't enough school places for Heworth's children and so Heworth formed a School Board to be responsible for providing extra school places. In all, between 1877 to 1883, they built six schools at Bill Quay, Low Felling, High Felling, Wardley Colliery, Felling Shore and Windy Nook.

When the Government abolished School Boards in 1902, responsibility for education was taken over by Felling Council who built a further four schools, one of which was Heworth Council school which for over 70 years occupied a prominent position on the site of what is today's Metro Interchange.

Left: A charity dance held at Heworth School 1922. Robert Sisterson (*see page 33*) of Felling is seated centre.

Miss Tradwell's class in 1904 in the hall of the new school. Note the portraits of King Edward VII and Queen Alexandra on the back wall.

The same hall 15 years later. The children have changed and so has the plant.

The school opened in May 1904 on land formerly owned by the North Eastern Railway Company as Heworth Council School thus replacing John Hodgson's old Heworth Parish School. The headmistress of the old school, Miss Jessie E. Gunn, became headmistress of the new school.

A new parish hall was built on the site of the old school which was entirely paid for by Felling's millionairess, Miss Emily Easton (*see page 33*) of Nest House. She provided £1,500 for its construction.

After this school was demolished in 1975 the children moved to a new school at The Drive.

In 1933, the first proposal for a secondary school at Heworth was made and the council applied for a grant of £42,300. This was at first refused but later agreed. In 1940, the Council were allowed to borrow £2,283 as payment for preliminary expenses incurred in preparatory plans for the new school. The war intervened and plans were disrupted. Eventually, it was Durham County Council who would build Heworth Grange Secondary School in the 1960s.

Left: Heworth School in the late 1930s. The same hall as in the images above but with new portraits of Queen Elizabeth and King George VI and another plant.

Right: Heworth School staff, c. 1946. Back row: Evelyn Menzies, unknown, Nellie Smith, Ethel Simpson, unknown. Front row: Mrs Graves, Mrs N. Richardson, Nancy Fewster, Mrs Ann Grove.

Below: A Christmas play performed in the late 1950s at Heworth Council School.

Right: The opening of the children's clinic on 3rd October 1925. A childrens clinic was established in a small bungalow beside the church which was described as a perfect little hospital in miniature. It contained one tiny ward with three beds, a theatre, bathroom, waiting room, consulting room, dental surgery and a nurses' room. Outside was a small garden. It was designed to be used for all school children in Felling Urban District and was the brainchild of Felling's Officer of Health, Dr Peacock. In the 1930s this little clinic was treating 800 children per month. Like the school, it was demolished in 1975.

To care for the community prior to the establishment of the National Health Service, Heworth had a Nursing Association which was maintained by subscriptions and employed a nurse. In 1914 between October and November she made a total of 703 visits to 70 cases.

To move patients, Heworth Colliery Ambulance (horse drawn) was originally used but in 1914 new rules meant that the ambulance could not leave the colliery so long as a miner was working underground. This meant that people were now asked to subscribe for a new ambulance. This began operating in 1915 although anyone actually wanting to use it first had to apply to a member of the committee with an application countersigned by the doctor. Members of the Nursing Association could have free use of the ambulance but everyone else had to pay at least ten shillings.

Bricks and Mortar

The church has already been mentioned but Heworth had other fine buildings – some of which are still here today.

Constitutional Club

In 1908, this became the Heworth, Pelaw, Felling and District Constitutional Club having started out life as the original vicarage. It was sandwiched between the Ship Inn and the Wheatsheaf public houses – roughly on the site of the long stay car park for the Metro today. The club contained a reading room, smoking room, games room, billiard room and a committee room together with accommodation for the caretaker. It was officially opened on 7th November 1908 by George Renwick, MP for Newcastle. Following the opening ceremony, 200 sat down to tea which was catered for by Jarrow Co-op Bakery. The building was demolished in 1959.

Heworth Hall

Heworth Hall was built in two stages on the site of an earlier farmstead. The oldest part (the north side) dates from about 1730 but further rooms were added on the south side later in the 18th century. This extension may have been done by the architect William Newton who designed similar halls in the North East.

The original building was constructed for William Russell of Sunderland and Brancepeth Castle. John Russell, a relative, later lived here and was always regarded as the Heworth squire. He is buried in Heworth churchyard. His daughter, Elizabeth Smart lived here until her death in 1866 as did her daughter, Elizabeth Shadforth, John Russell's granddaughter who died in 1872. It was later lived in by Samuel Meynell who owned Imeary's Chemical works on Heworth Shore.

The building was empty by the end of the First World War so the Vicar of St Mary's bought it as Heworth War Memorial Hall. The opening ceremony in September 1919 was preceded by a luncheon served in a marquee. The intention was that the hall was to be a parish centre and would provide a headquarters for demobilised soldiers and sailors together with a Women's Institute. The scheme cost £5,500 with substantial help promised from Heworth Colliery. However, the upkeep was prohibitive and the building was converted to a Conservative Club in 1929 after the sudden death of the Vicar. In 2011 this ceased and the hall is now occupied by a private business.

Heworth Hall, Grade II listed building, seen here in 1912.

White House

The White House, High Heworth, was regarded as one of the most rambling – and possibly the most haunted houses in the area. It was certainly an old house as it is mentioned in 1530. During the Civil War of the mid 17th century it was occupied by the Jennison family – a staunch Roman Catholic family. However, its most famous resident was Camilla Colville who became known as 'Camilla of the White House'. She became Countess Tankerville and a lady in waiting to Queen Caroline, wife of George III.

The house was advertised for sale by auction on 4th October 1810 when it was described as *'Delightfully situate in the centre of the estate. Abounds with game. Good freestone quarry on premises.'* The sale included the mansion house, gardens, shrubberies, large and commodious cold bath with a fine spring of water and dressing room attached – *'a good Farmhouse, Hind's House, Barns, Byers, Stables, and every other convenience, 260 acres, approximately, of rich Arable, Meadow and Pastureland.'*

The White House looking in poor condition prior to demolition.

From 1820, the house was occupied by Richard Carnaby Foster. It was last occupied in 1938 after which the house quickly became derelict and was eventually demolished in 1960.

Garden of Remembrance

Right: Garden of Remembrance, c. 1953. The Drive Primary School was later built on the site of the prefabs shown at the right of the photograph.

A garden of remembrance was created in 1953 as a memorial to the young men who lost their lives in both world wars. It was (and what remains of it) situated at the bottom of The Drive, near the site of the Low Heworth corn mill and was officially opened by Lord Lawson of Beamish in September 1953. Part of the site had previously been used by Felling Council to store the grit and ash needed whenever icy conditions prevailed on Sunderland Road.

There were two plaques in the garden. The first read: *'This garden is presented by members of the Felling Centre of the Women's Voluntary Service to the citizens of Felling in honoured memory of those from this area who gave their lives for their country in the Second World War 1939-1945.'*

The second read: *'This garden of remembrance dedicated to all those who gave their lives for their country and freedom was subscribed by the Felling Welcome Home and Memorial Fund on June 2nd 1953.'* This date was, of course, Coronation Day. Only the first plaque remains today to mark the spot of the garden.

The pre-fabs on The Drive were erected, not, as in many places, as a result of housing shortages caused by bomb damage but simply by a general housing shortage. These proved popular and many people were sad to see them go when they were demolished in 1973. Each contained a living room, kitchen, bathroom, two bedrooms. The kitchens were fitted with a cooker, cupboards and, amazingly for the time, a fridge.

Felling

'About half past eleven o'clock in the morning of 25th May 1812, the neighbouring villages were alarmed by a tremendous explosion at this colliery.' (Rev John Hodgson)

In 1812, Felling made the headlines. Colliery accidents were common but the explosion which occurred here in 1812 had far reaching consequences. It was the worst colliery accident in the history of mining up to that date.

A new seam at Felling opened in 1810 owned by the Brandlings, Henderson and Grace. The working pit was the John Pit situated on the north side of Sunderland Road between Felling toll bar and Felling Hall. The ventilation shaft was the William Pit situated 550 yards south west. The colliery was *'considered by the workmen a model of perfection in the purity of its air, and orderly arrangements ...'* (Rev John Hodgson). There had been no previous accidents.

Around 11.30am on Monday, 25th May 1812, a terrific explosion was heard which could be heard for nearly four miles. Huge quantities of dust and coal particles rose high in the air as fire broke from both pits and spread for a mile and a half covering Heworth so deeply that footprints could be made in the dust.

As soon as the explosion was heard, wives and children ran to the John Pit and men ran to turn the gin, attached to which was the rope, the steam engine normally used to raise men up and down the shaft having been destroyed in the blast. Against all odds, 32 men were rescued together with the bodies of two boys who had been badly burned. Sadly, three of those rescued, all boys, died later. One hundred and twenty one men were in the mine at the time of the explosion – 87 were still there.

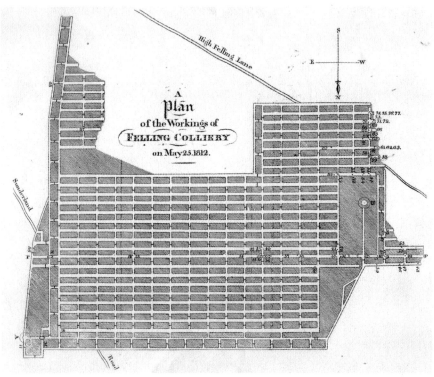

Plan of the workings of Felling Colliery, 25th May 1812.

The explosion had been caused by methane gas (fire damp) and a party of rescuers now had to try to go down with their only light coming from flint mills as a lighted candle would have caused a further explosion. The rescuers tried various routes to rescue the men but the poisonous atmosphere and the threat of a further explosion proved too much.

The following day it was announced that the shafts would be sealed so that the fire would burn itself out. This was met with dismay and even cries of *'Murder!'*

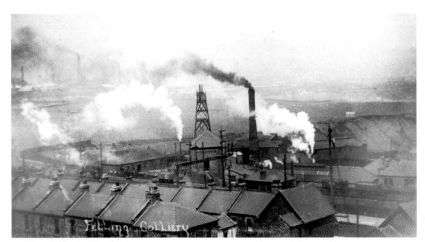

Felling Colliery in later years.

Many colliers from Wearside travelled to the pit and complained about the lack of effort being made to rescue the miners. So, on Wednesday 27th, two men, Mr Straker, the colliery viewer and Mr Haswell, the overman, went down into the John Pit for the second time. Their flint mill, the only source of lighting they had, was soon extinguished in the dank damp conditions and when Haswell was affected by the atmosphere, both men were forced to retreat. On their arrival at the top, they were greeted with cries of disbelief and so two others went down but once again were forced back by the fumes.

On Friday, 29th May, both pits were sealed with clay and straw. There was now no hope for those still underground.

The following week, preparations began to reopen the mines but these took time to complete as bore holes had to be constructed for ventilation. On the morning of Wednesday, 8th July at 6am, Mr Straker, Mr Anderson (an overman) and six others went down the William Pit. There they discovered their first body – in such a putrid state no one wanted to touch it. However, a coffin was lowered into which the body was put and drawn to the surface where a further 91 coffins were waiting.

Most of the relatives wanted their dead to lie in their homes but a doctor dissuaded them saying that this might cause an outbreak of putrid fever. Many of the men were so disfigured by the explosion that they could only be recognised by items of clothing or personal belongings. During July, an almost daily procession of coffins could be seen making their way to St Mary's Church.

One body, number 92, was never recovered. Number 91, the final body to be found was dug from under a heap of stones on Saturday, 19th September, four months after the explosion.

Four bodies, (numbers one, four, five and fifty) were buried in single graves. The others were interred in a trench side by side, two coffins deep with a partition of brick and lime between every four coffins.

Many local people contributed to the subscription fund which opened on 28th May. Collections were taken in other parish churches and by the end of the year £2,806 15s 6³/₄d had been taken.

John Hodgson preached a funeral service for the miners at St Mary's on Sunday, 9th August 1812. At that stage, 89 bodies had been recovered.

It was Hodgson's publicity of the Felling Pit disaster of 1812 which exposed for the first time the dangers of working underground (previously, disasters had been kept 'under wraps' by their owners) and led directly to the development of the miner's safety lamp. Hodgson wrote an account of the disaster which included the sermon he preached at the funeral service. He hoped that sales of this might go towards creating a memorial and a colliers' hospital. The memorial happened – the hospital didn't.

The memorial to those killed can be seen in the churchyard with a later blue plaque memorial fixed to the exterior of the wall.

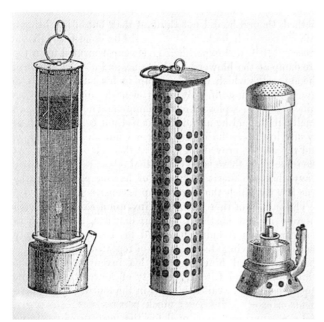

Above: Two types of safety lamp – Sir Humphry Davy's with gauze (*left*) and George Stephenson's which used glass (*right*) and a cover (*middle*).

Right: The memorial to the 91 men and boys whose bodies were recovered from the pit.

Health and Housing

When Felling got its own Local Board in 1868 (*see page 4*), it operated under the title of Felling Urban District Sanitary Authority. Twelve members were elected on 22nd August 1868 and held their first meeting two days later under the chairmanship of William Watson Pattinson of Felling Chemical works. William Hylton Dyer Longstaffe, a Gateshead solicitor, became their first clerk. On the 9th September they formed three separate committees concerned with sanitation, roads and finance.

In 1894, under the Local Government Act, this new authority became the Urban District Council of Felling. The first meeting of the new council was held on 7th January 1895 with the mining engineer, Alfred Septimus Palmer elected as chairman and the local board's accountant, George Bolam elected as their first clerk. Other appointments were largely carried over from the Sanitary Authority.

Sanitation had been one of the main reasons for Felling wishing to form a Local Board and, by the end of the 19th century, the problem was increasing. Most toilets where they existed were ash closets but even worse were the middens situated on Felling Shore and in areas around the railway line. These could remain full of stinking and decaying matter until eventually removed, often by a local farmer.

Felling refuse destructor.

In a letter to the Council, the Borough Surveyor, Charles Hall complained that as the refuse tips were now almost full, a new way of waste disposal was needed. He was asked to compare the cost of taking refuse out to sea with the cost of erecting a refuse destructor. It was this latter course that was agreed as the costs for both schemes were very similar but the refuse destructor had the advantage that waste could be disposed of on a daily basis. Also, the by-products of clinker and of steam were both useful.

The new-state-of-the-art destructor was formally opened on 3rd July 1906 by Councillor T.C. Major, Chairman of Felling Council. Designed by the Council Surveyor, Henry Miller, the destructor was situated beside what was described as a 'new road' (this became Abbotsford Road) on land purchased from Walter Scott's printing works. A 10 ton weigh bridge was constructed. The destructor was built of Pelaw bricks, with the exterior bricks being carefully dressed. At the same time, the Council decided to build new stables for their horses. Until then, all the horses used by the Council had been kept in hired stables. Four blocks of stables were built capable of housing 24 horses and the whole cost came to £11,180. Felling Council was rightly proud of its new refuse facility and opened it for public viewing on four separate days in August 1906.

The new stables and cart shed.

By the Second World War, the destructor was becoming obsolete and once empty, was used by the fire brigade for practice. It survived until the end of the 1970s as Abbotsford Road Council Depot.

Felling's first medical officer of health was Dr Michael Francis Kelly who produced his first annual report to the newly formed Felling Council in 1894. Although Dr Kelly was deeply concerned about some of the unsanitary and overcrowded conditions in which the poor had to live, he laid much of the blame for poor health on alcohol, lack of open air exercise, and eating insufficient meat. But his main concern was about the drinking of strong tea which he claimed affected the teeth and stomach. Women were particular sufferers. *'I believe the female side of an asylum has as many victims from over indulgence in this beverage as the male side has from indulgence in alcohol … a tea heart and a tobacco heart are now recognised complaints in the medical repertoire.'*

This is particularly ironic as the gifts presented to inmates of workhouses and asylums were invariably tea for women and beer for men! Dr Kelly was careful to note however that only tea which had brewed over five minutes was the culprit.

In the mid 1880s, Dr Kelly had to investigate an outbreak of gastro-enteritis. Usually when outbreaks like this occurred, the fault was often found in the old or stale food being hawked around the district. 'Fresh' herrings were often a particular culprit. On this occasion however, the blame seemed to lie with rabbits being sold on the streets and in the public houses by Ann Little, a poor female hawker. When Dr Kelly investigated her home, he was shocked to discover that the 'rabbits' were actually cats! A barrow of cat skins in her yard was all the evidence needed to convict her. During the case it was said that Ann was often under the influence of drink and had a son confined to a lunatic asylum. She was charged with stealing cats and also a game cock and fined 40 shillings. As she couldn't afford to pay this, she was sentenced to three months hard labour.

Dr Kelly pictured in the 1890s.

Dr Kelly also criticised the use of patent medicines such as those sold in the local drug stores or through adverts in the local papers which promised miracle cures. There were certainly no shortages of places in Felling where people could go for their health needs. In 1900, there were two bonesetters, two herbalists, one chemist and druggist and a drug store listed in the annual trade directory. Drug stores were not allowed to dispense medicine but could only supply branded products. Sisterson's on Felling High Street was one such although it later became a chemist's when Thomas Sisterson qualified as a pharmacist.

Dr Kelly died in 1902 and was succeeded by William Peacock who continued the good work of his predecessor throughout the district. He oversaw many improvements in health during his time in office, one of which was the gradual replacement of the old ash closets by more hygienic and efficient water closets.

In 1918, there were only 543 water closets as opposed to 4,147 ash closets and 23 ash pits. By the time of Dr Peacock's death in 1937, there were 5,982 water closets with only 170 ash closets and two ash pits still in existence.

Once the First World War ended, there was a general reaction to the wretched conditions that many servicemen were returning to. Some streets at what became known as High Felling had already been built in the early years of the 20th century. Coldwell Street, which up to then had contained only a few separate houses, now contained many more and a number of streets such as Woodlands Terrace and Hewitson Terrace had been built.

In 1919, a new housing act, the Addison Act, began the movement which ultimately led to the creation of council houses and Felling was an authority which had the vision to see how this could lead to improvements.

Felling Shore children in Tyne Street. Many are bare footed. An advert for Victory Tea is behind them.

Substantial grants were offered and although these were subsequently cut, further Acts in the 1920s provided more finance. These culminated in an Act of 1930 which obliged councils to demolish any slum housing and provided subsidies for new housing.

Felling Council embraced these Acts with the result that the Felling Shore district virtually disappeared and new estates at Bog House (the most prestigious estate laid out on garden city lines), Nest House and Felling House were all completed by the Second World War.

Bog House Estate was built on the site of Bog House Farm and on it was constructed Rectory Road, Chillside, Belgrave Terrace, Pitcherwell and Werehale Green. Once these streets had been built, others, such as Ell-Dene Crescent, Smithburn Road, Colepeth, Prestmede, Cotgarth, the south side of Watermill Lane and Thorney Garth, followed. The estate was designed by Charles Hall, the Council Surveyor, who liked the houses so much, he moved to one in Watermill Lane when it was completed even though the estate was meant to be occupied by the working classes. The street names were chosen by Charles Taylor, a member of Charles Hall's staff who had a keen interest in local history. He later became the rent collector for the estate.

Watermill Lane, Felling, 1930.

The estate was interesting as best quality materials were used for construction, there were a variety of housing styles and most streets were curved and spacious. They all had front and back gardens, fences, gates, and a built in coal house plus (a luxury undreamed of for many!) a bathroom with a flush toilet. Each had two or three bedrooms together with a living room, kitchen and separate pantry. The larger houses were usually built on the corner sites. Rents were very reasonable – a two bedroomed house on Cotgarth could be occupied for just 2s 9d per week in 1929.

In 1933, the Council announced that 139 houses were to be built at Stoneygate. Although they said they were borrowing £40,500 from the Ministry of Health, it was actually the Newcastle Savings Bank who put up the money at an annual 3% interest. It was intended that these new houses would only be for people from the slum clearance areas – largely Felling Shore. By January 1934, 38 were occupied with a further 20 completed and ready for tenants. They were built by a Darlington firm – L.W. Evans, although the Council complained that the firm were only employing 55% local labour as opposed to the 85% agreed. Names for the new streets, which largely reflected geographical features, were allocated in January 1934. Rents at Stoneygate ranged from 6/- per week for a bungalow to 10/6 for a four bedroomed house

On 18 June, 1938, Felling proudly declared the opening of their 2,000th council house. This was number 7 Green Lane Gardens, built on the Nest Estate. This was the estate originally owned and occupied by the Easton family but the house was demolished and the site sold to the Council in 1932. They paid £1,050 (which they borrowed from the Ministry of Health) for a little over 9,320 acres and used council labour to erect the houses. The show house (*see right*) was furnished by Ernie Walters who advertised bedroom suites from £10 10s and washers ranging in price from £2 15s to £7 5s. The show house remained open for three weeks.

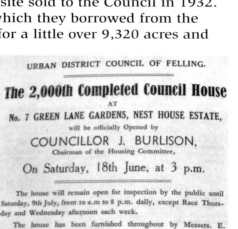

Official opening of 7 Green Lane Gardens, Nest House Estate.

'A delightful display of furniture' from Ernie Walters – furnishers of 7 Green Lane Gardens.

There were always waiting lists for these houses and often complaints that some people were managing to 'jump' the lists. In 1947, when there was a shortage of properties, there were accusations that *'the only way to secure a (council) house was to sit on the Councillor's doorstep.'*

Schooling

Improvements in education began in the late 19th century. Until then, schools in Felling were sporadic – one of the first schools was the school for children of the chemical workers at Felling Shore, always known as Lees School. When the works closed, the building became the first St John's RC School. A private school, Crow Hall Academy, was opened in Crow Hall by Dr William Grieve in 1839. This had a short life and closed in 1850 following Dr Grieves' marriage. After the Education Act of 1870 made education for all primary age children compulsory, Felling came under the Heworth School Board. High Felling Board School was the first to be built in 1877 and was situated on Stephenson Terrace on land bought from Bog House Farm. The building cost approximately £8,300 and could house 450 infants and 700 juniors. It was enlarged in 1891. Felling Shore Board School followed in 1882 – a much smaller building costing £1,900 and able to house 160 infants. This was situated near the foot of Stoneygate Lane and was nicknamed *'The tile-sheds school'*.

In the same year, Low Felling Board School opened at a cost of approximately £7,000. This was a two storey building (the others were single storey) able to house 295 infants and 530 juniors built opposite Mulberry Street. The summer house of Felling Hall remained in the school playground for many years until demolished in the 1920s.

School Boards were abolished in 1902 and education then became the responsibility of the Council. Under the new education committee, Falla Park Road Infant and Junior School opened on 14th April 1902. This is now the oldest school in the Felling area. The Council also opened St John's RC Secondary School in Willow Grove in 1936.

Children from the area who passed the Scholarship exam and later the 11 + examination, had to travel to Jarrow Secondary (later Grammar) School for their education. Secondary education came to Felling in the 1960s with the opening of Highfield School – this was later renamed Thomas Hepburn School in 1992.

Hard Times

As well as providing improved housing and education, members of Felling Council were also faced with trying to deal with the years of economic depression which lasted throughout most of the 1920s and 1930s. Both Heworth and Felling Collieries suffered partial closures (Felling Colliery closed for good in 1931) causing hardship to many. A welfare scheme provided hot breakfasts for poor children at school while there was a constant stream of similar schemes such as the annual footwear fund. The Council tried to help local businesses by reducing their rates but this then impacted on Council revenue. Sadly, many eviction notices were served on people unable to pay their rents while the means test (a scheme where the unemployed had to live off the sale of their excess furniture before being allowed to claim unemployment benefit) was universally detested. One Felling Councillor, the Communist James Ancrum (*see page 35*) fought the cause against both.

Despite the difficulties of the depression years, improvements continued to be made to benefit local people. A new recreation ground was created at Cotgarth on the Bog House Estate in 1935 which provided both bowling and putting greens, a new library was opened and the King George V playing field was constructed when Swards Road was completed in 1939. The recreation ground cost £1,455 and was opened by Councillor Oliver Henderson, himself an enthusiastic bowler. The first bowls match pitted the Police against members of Felling Park Bowling Club.

The library, a branch of Durham County Council, was formally opened on Saturday, 29th June 1935 by local historian John Oxberry. Situated on Gosforth

Flag Day for footwear from 1938.

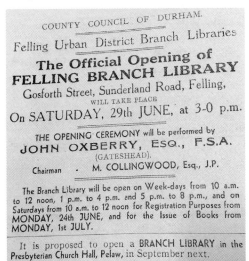

New library for Felling.

Street, it became well used and lasted until a new building was built on Tarlton Crescent (now demolished). A report of the time said: *'The library is as yet a novelty to children.'* However, it was certainly popular with others as 1,300 readers tickets were issued on the first day with several hundred more people on a waiting list.

This was the first time books could be borrowed by customers without charge. Previously, and for some time afterwards, there were a number of subscription libraries in existence. These included Potter's clothing store at Heworth who supplied 'latest modern fiction' courtesy of Foyles bookstores in London; Walton's newsagents in Pelaw and W. Dixon & Sons, newsagents on Crowhall Lane. The latter two charged 2d per book per week.

Felling at War

The First World War had little impact on Felling at first. The children's annual excursion in 1914, when over 1,000 children were taken to the seaside, still took place even though war had been declared the day before. Many men joined up and most initially were sent to soldiers' camps like the one on the postcard right.

This rather tongue in cheek postcard with clues to its location may have come from Felling but it is also possible that this was the Leam Camp at Heworth where various battalions of the Durham Light Infantry were stationed to begin their service. Training camps appeared throughout the British Isles and all new recruits were sent to one. Here they were drilled, marched and trained to use rifles and bayonets.

Almost immediately war was declared, Felling organised a War Distress fund. Within the first month, £264 15s 6d had been

Soldiers' camp, 1914.

collected. By the following month this figure had doubled and by May 1916, the fund had reached £2953 6s 7d. All kinds of fund raising was carried out. Simpsons the chemists on Felling High Street put a soldier's cap in their window to collect money *'to buy cigarettes for the soldiers'*, and it wasn't long before a variety of women's working parties sprang up and began knitting mufflers, jumpers, scarves and socks. These groups also, however, collected other things to send out – toilet soaps and cigarettes were popular and there were frequent requests from soldiers themselves for mouth organs and footballs.

To begin with, reports of fatalities were few. However, as the war progressed, the lists of dead reported grew in size. In 1916, three Felling men were lost at the Battle of Jutland – two on the 'Queen Mary' and one on the 'Invincible'. Another Felling man died on board the SS Hampshire – alongside Britain's great war hero Lord Kitchener.

As the war continued, things began to hit home. The childrens excursion in 1915 was cancelled *'owing to the inability of the railway company to grant special facilities due to military requirements.'* People were encouraged to save their waste such as papers, bottles, jam jars, old metal tins, tin and lead foil, cardboard, wood and wooden boxes.

The Council offices on Sunderland Road were used as a recruiting station and a Volunteer Training Corps (the equivalent of the later Home Guard) began in 1915.

Recruitment advert for the Volunteer Training Corps.

All men over military age were encouraged to enlist but at the first meeting held, when it was resolved to start the Corps, it was noted: *'Although it was decided to form a Volunteer Training Corps for the district, there was an absence of enthusiasm which must be regretted.'*

Planning for the Second World War began nearly two years before war was declared. In 1938, the local paper was advertising for Auxiliary Fire Service volunteers, ambulance drivers and air raid wardens while in May 1939, a recruiting march was held on behalf of Felling territorials. And in Felling Library, they had some ominous sounding new titles in stock: *'My quest for peace'*, *'I knew Hitler'* and *'Czechs and their minorities'*.

Schoolchildren were evacuated on the 8th and 9th September (about a week later than most other local areas) to Cumberland. Ellen Wilkinson, Felling's MP, made an appeal in the local newspaper for all mothers to evacuate their children: *'If a bomb should fall … and one of these children be killed who might have gone, the mother would never forgive herself.'* Despite this, however, within weeks, many had returned to their Tyneside homes.

Evening classes were cancelled but resumed again in the New Year. These were aimed at the over 14s (then the school leaving age) and adults. They were mostly practical courses, for example dressmaking and war time cookery for women and woodwork for men.

'It is wor effort for War effort' (Felling Council slogan)

As with the First World War, it wasn't long before the council were appealing for waste materials, including requests this time for bones and for the metal caps from electric lightbulbs. It wasn't long either, before the Chief Air Raid warden was complaining about wrongly installed Anderson shelters, gas masks being incorrectly carried in old Ostermilk tins, and children playing on, and consequently damaging, sandbags outside public air raid shelters. A community kitchen opened at High Felling School in 1941. This provided cooked food between 12 noon and 1.30pm every day except Sundays. People collected their food (a full meal cost 6d) and then took it home in their own containers. If they didn't want, or couldn't afford, the full meal, then some items were available separately.

During the war, Felling Town Hall became the headquarters for the Home Guard, Civil Defence, police and fire brigades and its telephone exchange was manned around the clock. Dempsterville House on Carlisle Street was taken over as offices of the Food Controller, Fuel Controller and Headquarters of the Auxiliary Fire Service.

The AFS made the news in 1941, not for their fire-fighting exploits, but because their then controller, a Felling Councillor, was convicted of the theft of 10 gallons of petrol and a tyre. He was sentenced to three months imprisonment and another Councillor hastily appointed to take his place.

Felling Auxiliary Fire Service, 1939.

An advert for the AFS, 17th May 1941.

Church services were held on Sunday evenings rather than afternoons. Cinemas initially closed but re-opened by October. Concerts by the Felling Male Voice Choir planned for Newcastle City Hall and Blackpool were cancelled as was Felling Amateur Operatic Society's performance of 'The Country Girl'.

Public air raid shelters (capacity in brackets) were built at Church Place (100), foot of The Drive (150), Rectory Road (50), Elliott Street (200), Neville Street (100), Bondene Avenue (100), The Drive (100) and Hopper Road (200). Trenches (underground shelters) were built at Falla Park, High Felling, Windy Nook and St John's Schools, with schools not able to open until these had been completed.

Shops closed early on Mondays to Thursdays at 6pm, on Friday 7pm and Saturday 7.30pm. However, confectioners and tobacconists were allowed to stay open later.

Shelters were advertised for sale in 1940 on easy terms – an initial payment of £1 5s followed by ten monthly payments of 12s 6d. You saved money if you could pay the full amount in one go – £6 14s.

The Council provided 272 allotments and provided lots of advice about how and when to grow vegetables saying *'while flowers are pleasing to the eye, they are unsatisfactory to the palate.'*

They also established a demonstration allotment under the supervision of the County Horticultural Superintendent and under a county allotments scheme were able to provide seed potatoes and fertiliser at reduced prices.

Left: Felling Park staff in the 1940s.

Felling Councillors and officials pictured after the Second World War. Note the symmetrical crossing of the legs!

The war affected Felling Council's improvement programme – not just the duration of it but what had to be done after it. Air-raid shelters, had to be demolished and gas masks collected. Roads had been tank damaged, buildings and outdoor spaces had been filled with trenches and the grass verges had been damaged by smoke screen stoves. These repairs all cost money which the Council could ill afford and consequently rates were increased. This proved an unpopular move which eventually led to the formation of the Rent and Ratepayers Party.

Snapshot of Shopping

Felling had a variety of good shops on both the High Street and Sunderland Road, although shopping on the High Street could be fraught with danger – shops (and shoppers) were always at risk from runaway horses and carts and, later, motorised vehicles.

Above: A view down Felling High Street, c. 1910. The first shop on the left is Costelloe's pawnbrokers with its distinctive golden balls.

Right: A 1930s advert for McGuinness stores. Their family department store 'Felling House' occupied a prime position of the High Street and is shown on the photograph above near the centre of the picture on the left hand side. The store closed in 1939.

Left: Thompson's butchers shop, c. 1920s. Mr Thompson, Margaret Henderson and Alfie Eales are shown outside the shop in Crowhall Lane, Felling.

Above: T.P. Heslop's butchers shop. Felling was well served by butchers – others included Myers pork shop and Robinson's.

Left: Smith's greengrocers, 9 High Street, in the 1920s.

Nichol's shoe shop in 1923 advertising *'High class boot repairs without nails or sewing'*. Left to right: Charles Nichols, Ted Jones, J.W Lavender, J. Nichol (owner).

Ramsay and Son watchmaker and jeweller, Felling, 1920. Ramsay was the grandson of Tommy Ramsay, the 19th century miners' leader from Pelton Fell.

Walter Willson's at the bottom of the High Street. This shop was converted from a Wesleyan chapel in the 1890s. The firm stayed in Felling until the 1960s. One of their popular products was 'Daisy' flour.

If the boots you are wearing
Stand in need of repairing,
 And you want them done natty and neat,
There's a shop in the Square,
Just take them straight there,
 And you'll get them done reasonably cheap.

Ladies' from 2/-. Gents' from 3/-.

Note the Address:

G. W. MOSES,

Victoria Square, Felling

A 1916 advert for G.W. Moses shoe shop. This was one of the longest established shops in Felling. During the Boer War they produced hand-made boots for soldiers. The shop closed when Felling town centre was re-developed in the 1970s.

SEE OUR WINDOWS
E. WALTERS & SON, 35 HIGH STREET, FELLING
HOUSE FURNISHERS,

A 1930s advert for Ernie Walters. This store was first established by Ernie's grandfather who started a furniture store on Davidson Street in 1862. Ernie became a well-known Felling tradesman whose goods were often used to furnish the 'show house' on the new council estates (*see advert on page 26*). The firm was later taken over by his son, Stan and became one of the oldest firms to trade on the High Street. Ernie must have done well out of his business as he could afford to sail on the maiden voyage of the 'Queen Mary' to America in 1936.

People of Felling

Thomas Hepburn – 'Felling's first trade unionist' (1796-1864)

Born at Pelton, Thomas Hepburn began working at Urpeth Colliery when he was only eight. As a young man, he joined the Primitive Methodists and became a good public speaker. In 1831, he founded the Northern Union of Pitmen – 'the Pitmen's Union of the Tyne and Wear' and brought the men out on strike in order to improve working hours, the 'tommy shop' system and to stop the annual bond. He won concessions but in 1832, when further action was demanded, the mine owners were ready for a stoppage. The strike failed and Hepburn was forbidden work in any colliery. He tried to set up a small school and even went round the doors selling tea. Eventually, he was given a job at Felling Colliery on condition he took no further part in union activities. A peaceable law abiding man, he is the only 'local' to have featured on a postage stamp.

Right: Thomas Hepburn's grave, St Mary's Heworth.

Emily Matilda Easton – 'Felling's millionairess' (1818-1913)

Emily Matilda Easton lived all her life at Nest House – the house her father, Thomas Easton a colliery owner, had built at Felling Shore when he moved the family there from Ryton in about 1818. The house was a plain building surrounding by collieries and waste heaps but he built a fine garden and a private carriage road which ran from Sunderland Road to the house. As well as collieries, the Eastons owned much property in the area and became the richest family to live in the Heworth township. Emily owned substantial shares in both Bedlington and Wallsend and Hebburn Coal Companies.

When Emily died at Nest House on Christmas Day 1913, she left a vast fortune – £1,079,780 3s 3d. In her Will, she left substantial sums to charities including local hospitals and orphanages. Over the years, Dr Steel at St Mary's, Heworth, had been the beneficiary of regular gifts – many of which paid for the decoration of the church during his incumbency. It was estimated that throughout her life time Emily gifted £100,000 to local churches which included money provided for restoration works at St Nicholas' Cathedral in Newcastle. She both gifted and endowed St Chad's Church in Bensham and it was there that her funeral service was held.

Robert Sisterson – 'Felling's oldest tradesman' (1850-1932)

Robert Sisterson was born in Charlton Row, Felling and attended Lees School. He became an office boy at the chemical works when he was 12 and then served an apprenticeship with a Gateshead painter. He had just finished his apprenticeship when his father died suddenly and he took over his father's herbalist's business subsequently establishing his own painting business. He was a hard worker, often working 14 hours a day. He became president of the local Tradesmen's Association and was also president of the Property Owners and Ratepayers Association as well as president of the Master Painters Association. His son Stuart managed the paint and wallpaper shop while his other son Tom became a chemist and managed the chemist's shop next door (*see title page*). Robert died at his home, 5 Belgrave Terrace, on 21st May 1932 aged 82. His funeral was held at Heworth.

Robert Sisterson (left) with his son Stuart outside the family's decorators shop on Felling High Street.

The Dragone family – 'Felling's ice cream makers'

Above: Frances and Dominic Dragone in the 1930s.

Right: An advert for Dragone's ice cream. Dominic was a Felling stalwart, helping to found Felling Rotary Club in the late 1950s and fellow Rotarians formed a guard of honour at his funeral at St Patrick's Church. His father Giuseppe began making ice cream in a small shop on the High Street after the First World War but in the 1930s, he moved to Coldwell Street, opposite the Corona Cinema. The firm won many gold medals for their quality ice creams and the Dragone's ice cream van was a common and popular sight on Felling's streets. The family also had an accordion band.

Paul Cavanagh – 'Felling's Hollywood star' (1888-1964)

Real name Willie Atkinson, his father, William, was a grocer who had a shop on Coldwell Street and his uncle was Robert Sisterson. He attended the Royal Grammar School in Newcastle and was a scholar at the Wesleyan Sunday School. As a young man, he taught at the High Council School in Felling but later emigrated to Canada becoming a member of the Northwest Mounted Police. He first performed as an actor in a play at Croydon in 1924.

In films, he was usually seen in a supporting role although he was Mae West's leading man in ''Goin' to Town' in 1935. He appeared in three Sherlock Holmes films starring Basil Rathbone and Nigel Bruce in the 1930s and '40s. He made his last film 'The Four Skulls of Jonathan Drake' in 1959.

Above: 'Curtain at Eight' shown at the Imperia in 1934.

Ellen Wilkinson – 'Felling's feisty MP' (1891-1947)

Ellen was MP for the Jarrow constituency (which included the Felling area) from 1935 until her death in 1947. However, even before being elected, she was a frequent visitor to Felling. In 1933, she visited the New Labour Hall on Coldwell Street, Felling to lecture on her recent political trip to India and in 1935, as the prospective parliamentary candidate, she addressed an audience in the new Imperia cinema when she was described as *'a candidate lacking neither in ability nor earnestness.'*

Left: Ellen Wilkinson on Felling High Street in the 1930s.

Right: May Day celebrations in 1938. While MP, she provided a regular column in the local newspaper about Parliamentary affairs. On Saturday, 7th May 1938 she marched alongside others from Oakley's Field, Windy Nook to Heworth via Felling in a procession of bands, banners and tableaux. Later that year, on 23rd October, she and fellow MP Herbert Morrison attended a *'monster meeting'* at the Imperia.

There was genuine sadness when Ellen's death was recorded on 6th February 1947 and a memorial service was held for her at the Zion Congregational Church, Smithburn Road. As a later tribute, Felling's early 1950s council estate at Wardley was named the Ellen Wilkinson Estate.

James Ancrum – 'Felling's Communist Councillor' (1898-1946)

Left: James Ancrum speaking at a National Unemployed Workers Movement rally outside the Corona Cinema in Felling Square in the 1930s. The demands on the placards are for free milk and boots for the children of the unemployed and the placard in front of him proclaims *'Read the Daily Worker'*.

A Felling lad who once sold the local newspaper, 'Heslop's Local Advertiser', James Ancrum became a member of the Communist party in 1926. He first stood for election to Felling Council in 1931 but was unsuccessful. However, in 1935 he was elected to the Council by a large majority in a by-election. Ancrum joined the Royal Naval Reserve during the First World War when he was only 16 and served in the Second World War as an ARP warden. He led a national unemployed march to London in 1930.

Ancrum became a champion for those threatened by eviction and became a popular orator frequently speaking about the Means Test of which he was a strong critic. He headed the Felling branch of the National Unemployed Workers Movement becoming national organiser in the late 1930s. He died suddenly after a serious operation in 1946 at the comparatively early age of 47.

The Rev Gerard Nesbitt – 'Felling's quiet hero' (1911-44)

Born in Felling, he attended St Cuthbert's grammar school in Newcastle and studied for the priesthood at Ushaw College, Durham and the Venerable English College in Rome. He was a popular priest and loved by everyone whatever their religion. He served as a curate in Morpeth and joined the army in 1940. He was attached to the 8th battalion DLI and was soon posted to Cyprus and from there to the Middle East. He was present at all the battles fought by his battalion including El-Alamein and was twice recommended for the Military Cross, awarded the Croix de Guerre and also mentioned in dispatches. He was killed by a stray shell while burying the dead on 5th July 1944 when he was only 33 and was buried in Jerusalem War Cemetery, Chouain.

Windy Nook

The small area of Windy Nook has a full and interesting history populated with stories of heroism, philanthropy, sporting exploits and even murders. Although the basic layout of a village at a crossroads remains today, there is now very little trace of its earlier appearance and the people who lived here 100 years ago.

Windy Nook is well named as its hilly location at a cross roads, ensures that it is often a very windy spot! In 1858, it was described as *'a bleak village standing near the summit of a steep hill'* and it was still being referred to as that 70 years later. Often simply referred to as 'the Nook', its name first appears in a baptismal record for Dorothy, daughter of Richard Laws *'of Windie Nook'* in 1698. John Oxberry, the noted antiquarian and historian, surmises this may have been the name of a farm which subsequently gave its name to this small settlement.

The Windy Nook we know today was once part of Heworth common and an 18th century visitor would have discovered only a small scattering of haphazardly arranged cottages. When Heworth's four main landowners, John Colville, Charles Brandling and Jacob and Joseph Wilson, successfully petitioned Parliament to enclose and divide Heworth Common, the area of ground containing these cottages was left alone. From this inauspicious beginning, Windy Nook developed.

Throughout the 19th century, this little settlement gradually expanded until by 1900, it had a network of short streets. At the centre of the village was the Co-op where 'Windy Neukers' shopped, accumulated their 'divi' (dividend) and gossiped.

Sometimes, this gossip was of a dark nature. In 1907, it centred on the store itself – the scene of an infamous murder which made national headlines – not simply because of the crime but because of the story which unfolded around it.

The crossroads – the junction of Albion Street with Coldwell lane. The Black House can be seen at the left.

Church Row. The Post Office can be seen in the centre.

A Snapshot of 1901

In 1901, most people who lived here had been born in the area while others came from mining villages in County Durham. Virtually 90% of the male population in Windy Nook worked in either the stone quarries or coal mining. However, all trades were needed to make a village, so, there was a button-hole maker, stocking knitter, French polisher, chapel keeper, drug and drysaltery packer, dairyman, fishmonger, blacksmith, market gardener, telegram messenger, photographic and dry plate workers, school teachers, clergymen and publicans, and, of course, the resident policeman.

There were five public houses, one church, two Methodist chapels, a school, Mechanics' Institute, and farms. You bought your food at corner shops and at the Co-op and living in an upstairs flat meant you paid a weekly rental of about six shillings. If you caught one of the many infectious diseases then current, you might be sent to the fever hospital otherwise you were dependent on remedies obtained at the chemists – although you had to travel to Felling to find one.

It's Murder in Windy Nook!

In October 1907, it was realised that systematic pilfering was taking place in the Co-op's butchery department. The Co-op committee, with a misguided sense of justice, decided to catch the criminal(s) themselves rather than inform the police. In retrospect, this was the worst decision they could have made.

On Thursday, 31st October, three members of the committee, George Ather, Christopher Carr and John Patterson, together with a young butcher, John Cowell, settled themselves in the store ready for a night long vigil. Shortly before 10pm, Mr Sutton, the manager, left the building making a great show of locking and bolting the doors and turning the lights off. Inside, John Cowell carefully locked the door on the inside, pocketing the key, while a string was attached to the gas pendant ensuring the light could be switched on quickly.

Central branch store on Union Street, the scene of the murder.

All was quiet apart from a moment when the watchers heard the sound of the lock being tried but this was only the local policeman on his beat. Then about 4am, the street lamp outside the store went out. The men tensed – this, they thought, was the moment when the thief would strike.

Shortly after, they heard the sound of a key being inserted and turned in the lock. The men watched in silence as a man crossed the shop, made his way to the slaughterhouse, then returned with his theft. He was immediately seized by Patterson and Carr as Cowell pulled the string on the gas light illuminating the room.

During the violent struggle which followed, Carr let go of the burglar and, picking up a butcher's steel, struck him on the head. Patterson protested, telling Carr not to be violent. But then events took a turn for the worse.

Cowell suddenly shouted to the others: *'Look out – he's got a revolver in his hand!'*

Almost immediately, a shot rang out and Patterson fell, shot in the forehead. Another shot followed and Carr was hit in the hip. In the resultant confusion, Cowell ran for the police while Ather held the door from the outside to prevent the man's escape. Ather's house was very near the Co-op and the noise woke his wife who, hurriedly putting on a petticoat, ran to the store. She realised the intruder was trying to climb out of the window so ran back to the house to get an axe. Whilst there, she heard the crash of glass as the intruder broke out of the window. Ather seized a hammer and ran round to the window, struck him twice but was unable to prevent his escape. He ran after him and his wife, seeing what was happening, also joined in the chase. However, they lost him when he disappeared into the darkness of the nearby quarries.

John Patterson, the first man shot, died after two hours. Carr was taken to the Royal Victoria Infirmary, Newcastle, where the bullet was removed but he never fully recovered.

The survivors gave the police a description of a man wearing a slouch hat and a false beard, carrying a stout stick.

The search was now on to find the murderer and it wasn't long before a local blacksmith, Joseph William Noble was arrested. There was some damning evidence – he had two recently inflicted wounds on his head and another wound on the back of his leg. His house in Stone Street was then searched and yielded up some surprising finds.

John Patterson.

As well as skeleton keys, a lantern, revolver, cartridges, and a set of false whiskers, police also found keys to every lock and padlock in the Windy Nook store. They also discovered, behind a locked door, over 200 new goods – most of which were stolen from the Co-op including mustard, polish, soap, suits, and 114 new pairs of boots & shoes.

Noble was tried at Durham Assizes in March 1908 and although he protested his innocence, he was found guilty of murder and hanged at Durham on 24th March 1908. John Patterson's funeral service was held in the Ebenezer Chapel (of which he was a trustee and a longstanding member) where his coffin was taken in front of a packed crowd from his house in Paradise. Following the service, he was buried in St Alban's churchyard in front of a huge audience.

The Windy Nook Murder!

Joseph William Noble was found guilty, at Durham Assizes on March 8, of the murder of John Patterson at Windy Nook, and he was sentenced to death. The High Sheriff of Durham has fixed the execution for March 24.

DESPERATE AFFAIR AT WINDY NOOK.

Man Shot Dead and Another Injured.

Terrible Struggle with a Disguised Shopbreaker.

Windy Nook, a small village on the brow of the hill between Felling and Sheriff Hill, was early yesterday morning the scene of a tragedy, desperate in its character, and resulting in the death of one man and injury to a second by the revolver shots of a disguised shopbreaker. The cause of the tragedy was extremely simple, and it was extraordinary to think that a life should have been sacrificed over so little. During the past three weeks meat has been stolen several times at night time from Windy Nook Co-operative Stores, and as the pieces taken were large,

Above: Report of the crime in Newcastle Daily Journal, 2nd November 1907.

Left: The result of the trial, 8th March 1908.

Fifty years later, Windy Nook was again the scene of not just one murder but very probably four – all committed by the same rather innocuous looking pensioner. Within the space of four years, Mary Wilson managed to dispose of three husbands and her lodger, for the most part, without arousing suspicion.

Mary's first husband, John Knowles, died in 1955. This wasn't a surprise as the couple had been married for over 40 years, but when the live-in lodger, John Russell (with whom Mary had had a long standing affair), died within five months, a few eyebrows began to be raised. In both cases, Mary had reported their apparent illnesses to the local doctor who had prescribed medication which Mary had remarked to her neighbours *'didn't seem to be working'*. John Russell left Mary £46 pounds in his will but this wasn't enough for Mary who decided to look around for a new husband. She set her sights on Oliver James Leonard, a retired estate agent from Hebburn and they were married in September 1956. Less than a fortnight later, Oliver too was dead, with Mary collecting £50 from his insurance. Apparently she joked with the undertaker that as she was putting so much business his way, he should give her a bargain price!

Mary Wilson, the widow of Windy Nook.

Mary now needed to decide what to do next. So far, she had disposed of three men for fairly meagre returns. She waited 13 months before her last victim, Ernest George Lawrence Wilson, was selected. Ernest was a retired engineer with £100 invested in the Co-op, and a paid up insurance policy. They were married in October 1957 and Mary moved into his house. At the wedding reception, she was heard to say that the leftover cakes should be saved as *'they will come in quite handy for the funeral when he pegs out'.* Ernest lasted just 15 days.

The finger of suspicion was now firmly pointed at Mary. She had called in a new doctor to see Ernest who, becoming suspicious after discovering the patient had been dead some hours before Mary contacted him, ordered the other bodies to be exhumed. It was found that all contained traces of phosphorous, commonly found in rat poison. Mary had apparently administered this to her victims disguised in their tea.

Mary was tried for the murder of her last two husbands and was sentenced to death. However, due to her advanced age, this was commuted within five days to a life sentence. Four years later, she died in prison – from natural causes.

People of Windy Nook

Fortunately, Windy Nook has also had some rather more upright characters.

The man who arguably did most for his fellow Windy Nookers was probably John Oxberry, a quarryman, a former Chartist and a true Victorian 'son of toil'. He was the man behind Windy Nook's Mechanics' Institute and the formation of Windy Nook Co-operative Society. He supported Joseph Cowen in agitating for voting rights for the working man during the Northern Reform Union in 1858.

John Oxberry had the idea of starting reading rooms – somewhere where the local workers (mostly quarrymen like himself) could go, and where they could read and chat without the temptation of drink. The men began to subscribe a monthly fee and by 1859 they were able to rent two rooms in a house in Stone Street with John Oxberry using his donkey and cart to bring wood for seating and tables. The reading-rooms were successful and soon the membership had far outstripped the space available.

John Oxberry (1822-1893).

It was decided that a purpose built Mechanics' Institute was the only answer. A site of waste land beside an old half-filled quarry was built and Richard Wellington Hodgson, the quarry owner, gave the stone for the foundations, steps, lintels and sills. Night after night, after the 18 founder members had finished work, they toiled at dressing and shaping the stones. They appointed two Felling masons to build the Institute and the new building opened on Christmas Day 1861. Over 500 people had tea to celebrate the opening with entertainment from Felling band.

Left: Mechanics' Institute (this later became the Windy Nook & Carr Hill Club). John Oxberry's son, John, the local historian, later noted that his father's aim was for the building *'to be a centre of light and leading for the folks of Windy Nook.'* Lectures and classes took place there as well as entertainment. One of the best known entertainers was Geordie Ridley (author of 'Blaydon Races') who performed his local songs here in June 1863 to an audience of 300. However, times and tastes change and in 1913, the building was converted to a social club.

John Lindsay McCutcheon Brown-King is another notable person from Windy Nook. According to a contemporary newspaper report, by his own admission, he fired the first shot of the First World War for the British and with his second shot, shot down the German flag. John was a young Royal Marine serving on board the SS 'Amphion'. Just 32 hours after Britain declared war on Germany, the 'Amphion' sank a German minelayer, the 'Konigen Louise'. In an ironic twist of fate, the 'Amphion' later struck one of the mines laid by the 'Konigen Louise' and had to be abandoned. Many men died or were severely burned. One of the most severely injured was John Brown-King who, although escaping injuries from the original explosion, then suffered horrific injuries when he was caught in the second explosion while trying to help a fellow sailor enveloped in flames. He was rescued and taken to Shotley Naval Hospital, Harwich, where he lingered for two weeks before dying of his wounds. That was just long enough for his mother to make the long journey to see him.

John Brown-King was the first reported war death in the local newspaper, Heslop's Local Advertiser, but sadly, many others would quickly follow. Rolls of honour were printed showing all the 'old boys' from the local schools who had joined up and there were frequent fund raising efforts to supply them with comforts at the front. The Vicar of St Alban's, the Rev T.H.A. Morris, was secretary of the local War Relief Fund.

Brass memorial plaque in St Alban's Church commemorating John Brown-King.

Windy Nook Co-op

The Co-op movement is generally believed to have begun with the Rochdale Pioneers in 1844. Thirty years later and the first entry in the first minute book of Windy Nook Co-operative and Industrial Society includes a note about the beginnings: *'A few friends met accidentally ... when the question was asked ... Could we not have a store in our village?'*

A further friendly talk was held in the Mechanics' Institute and then a meeting was held at which the audience decided *'To form a co-operative society in the village.'* Business opened in a small shop on 14th August 1874 with John Oxberry as the first president and a board of trustees.

Right: The Society's first shop in Windy Nook.

Staff at the central branch.

Opening of the Co-op branch on Windy Nook Road on 12th March 1921.

Co-operative Crescent.

Following a dispute with the landlord over payment of rates, the Society then managed to build their own shop which opened in July 1876 on Union Street. It wasn't long before these premises were extended and by 1920, the Society had three branches – Springwell, Sheriff Hill and a second store at Windy Nook. In 1924 another branch opened at High Heworth.

The Society also bought a field on the west side of Coldwell lane and in November 1891, a contract was given to Robert Davidson, builder, to build cottages for members. The ballot to allot the cottages took place on 17th May 1892 with a guide price of about £175 and a minimum yearly payment of £12. Each successful member then had seven days in which to pay a deposit. Twelve houses were built and six years later, building started on 13 more. They were named Co-operative Terrace.

Co-operative Crescent was also built and later the Society built a street of flats named St Alban's Crescent but these were for anyone – the Co-op merely acted as landlord and collected the rents. In line with the ideals of the early Rochdale Pioneers, they also developed eight allotments to be tended by members and set up a penny bank.

In 1959, the society lost its name when it amalgamated with the Felling Shore, Heworth and Bill Quay Society. Ten years later, it became part of the Newcastle Co-operative Society.

Left: The Post Office on Church Row. Note the adverts for Cadbury's cocoa and chocolate. This photo probably dates from around 1910.

The Post Office opened in the mid 1890s replacing a nearby post box in the wall of Church Street. When first established there were two collections and deliveries each day. It was demolished in the 1970s.

Right: Albion Street – Note the Fry's advert displayed to match the angle of the gable roof!

Albion Street was part of one of the two original roads created by the 18th century enclosure award. Why it was given the name Albion remains a mystery.

The first houses in Windy Nook were largely demolished in a 1930s slum clearance programme although not all their residents wanted them to disappear. Streets with wonderful names such as Square Houses, Paradise Place and Sandmill Row all went, to be replaced with terraces making more economic use of the space available. The early little stone built cottages were arranged haphazardly and were described at an inquiry held at the time of their proposed demolition as looking as if they had been *'dumped down on the open ground without, apparently, any former planning or consideration of arrangement at all. There are groups of houses muddled together, standing at various heights and running at various angles from each other.'* Many of them had been built by the quarry workers, very often adjacent to old quarry workings. They had rubble stone walls which became very damp.

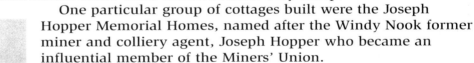

One particular group of cottages built were the Joseph Hopper Memorial Homes, named after the Windy Nook former miner and colliery agent, Joseph Hopper who became an influential member of the Miners' Union.

Left: Joseph Hopper (1856-1909). When only 18, Joseph Hopper became a Methodist lay preacher. He worked as a miner and colliery agent and became an active member of the Durham Miners' Association, the Felling Local Board and Durham County Council. Hopper can be regarded as the instigator behind the aged miners' homes. He brought the idea to the annual meeting of the Miners' Permanent Relief Fund in 1894 where he moved a motion *'That it be an instruction to the executive committee to devise some scheme for aged miners' homes.'* At the time, once a miner ceased working, he was evicted from his home. Hopper thought this unfair. In order to provide special retirement homes a small weekly levy was deducted from their wages. The movement grew and by 1914 nearly 500 homes had been built.

Right: Mr and Mrs Lisgo from Wardley Colliery were among the first tenants to move into the new Joseph Hopper Homes. Pictured here, left to right are: Mrs Lisgo, Mr Lisgo, John (unknown) and Bridget (unknown).

Joseph Hopper was a popular man – a local poem written during his life ran:

> *In the evening of life*
> *It has pleased God to send*
> *In you, Mr Hopper,*
> *The old Miners' friend*

He is buried in St Alban's churchyard and a memorial was erected to him in 1925. On it he is described as: *'A working man endowed with intellectual and executive powers of a rare order.'*

Quarries and Quarrymen

Running through Windy Nook was a wagonway, known as the Great Grindstone Way which ran from Washington to staithes at Felling Shore, carrying some of the huge grindstones produced from the numerous local quarries. The men who worked in these quarries laboured long and hard and in 1854, won a notable victory for a nine hour day – 16 years before this came into general acceptance. They then had even more success in 1874 when they won the right for an eight hour day.

Some of the men who worked at Windy Nook quarries.

By the beginning of the 20th century, the quarries were employing over 200 men. One of the earliest quarries in the Heworth district was established by Richard Kell which was well into production by 1784. The family continued the industry right through the 19th century and won awards at the Great Exhibition of 1851 and a gold medal at the Paris exhibition of 1885.

As well as being used to build St Alban's Church, the Ebenezer Chapel, the local board school and the fever hospital, Windy Nook stone was used to build Armstrong College in Newcastle, the Miners' Hall at Durham and the Shipley Gallery in Gateshead. The quarries later became run down and their sites were filled in during the 1960s. The quarries here were known as the blue quarries and they produced the highest quality of stone.

Quarry workers. This shows the sheer size of these huge grindstones – almost as tall or taller than the men. Accidents were common but not just to the quarry workers – unwary people walking in the dark could easily fall into them and be seriously injured.

Pits, Pubs and Pulpits

Coal was transported to the staithes by the Heworth wagonway which joined the Ouston and Pelaw wagonway and from there to staithes at Pelaw. Windy Nook miners worked at Heworth Colliery (*see page 10*) in the 19th and 20th centuries. There had been even earlier collieries however. The Sward Pit (Nursery Lane) and the Willie Pit located north of Albion Street were both working during the late 17th century and 18th century. Even when worked out, however, problems could remain and in 1914, plans for building houses had to be delayed due to the old coal workings of the Willie Pit.

During the miners' strike of 1912 there was great hardship throughout the country and St Alban's parish hall was used as a soup kitchen. It opened on 27th March 1912 and closed 24 days later on 23rd April. During that time the women here served a total of 5,200 meals – an average of nearly 217 per day. £17 6s 6½d was given as subscriptions together with 145 loaves of bread and varying amounts of meat, stock, bones and vegetables. Total expenses were £18 10s 11d leaving a deficit of 14s 5d.

To serve the needs of its workers, often involved in hard manual labour, Windy Nook had a comparatively large number of public houses of which only two, the Bay Horse and the Fiddlers Three (originally a colliery pub, the Ravensworth Arms) are still operating although the latter has been rebuilt. One other remains, but in a different guise and this is the Black House.

A miner's family at Windy Nook.

Above: The Black House Inn in the 1920s (now converted to a Tesco Express store). This has had various names including the Coal Waggon, and may have been rebuilt after a fire in 1844. In 1766 it is marked on a plan as belonging to Mary Robson. In the early 20th century, a bowling alley was situated behind the Black House.

Throughout the 19th century, the Black House was used for meetings of the Heworth Miners' Lodge who stored their banner upstairs, bringing it out for meetings, demonstrations and, of course, the annual Durham Miners' Gala.

Other public houses which were once a feature of Windy Nook life included the Hope and Anchor at the top of Coldwell Lane, the Hare and Hounds, the Crown and Thistle and the Engine House.

Right: The Hare and Hounds.

To serve the good of men's souls as well as their thirst, religion took a central part in this small area.

Right: St Alban's Church. Matthew Plummer, the Vicar of Heworth, began pressing for a new church at Windy Nook in order to halt the rise of Methodism. The church, a fairly plain building, later described as *'too cheap to be offensive'*, cost £875 18s and could seat 300. It opened in 1842 and when Plummer gave the first sermon he was so emotional that his wife later wrote that he

'entirely broke down while reading the lesson, and had to make many long pauses to recover himself before he could finish.'

The first incumbent was a young man of 25, Edward Hussey Adamson. Appointed as Curate in 1842, he became Vicar when St Alban's was created as a new parish and thus separate from Heworth in 1843. In 1846, he was married at St Alban's to Anne Potts of Carr Hill. At first the new family lived at Cleasby's Farm as the vicarage wasn't built until 1856. Adamson's yearly salary was only £135 – fortunately, in view of his large family, he also had a private income. He remained as Vicar until his death aged 81 in 1898 – a remarkable period of office of 56 years. In the churchyard are two sadly damaged gravestones to him and his wife and in the church are two windows in their memory. This gentle and unassuming clergyman and his family won the hearts of the local people by their many acts of kindness.

Left: The Adamson family, c. 1861. Shown here are Edward Hussey Adamson, his wife Anne and their seven children, Cuthbert, Anne, Emily, Eleanor, Edward, Katherine and the baby, Mary. Looking after the family and living in the Parsonage with them were four servants – a housemaid, nurse, cook and washerwoman. None of the last four girls ever married and both sons became vicars. Mrs Adamson died suddenly in 1873.

To celebrate Adamson's 50 years of service at St Alban's, it was decided to improve the church and the work was given to Adamson's son-in-law, the Newcastle architect W.S. Hicks (later to be the architect of the magnificent St Chad's Church in Bensham) who had married Ann, Edward's eldest daughter. Old pews were removed and a new pulpit and chancel screen erected.

The churchyard houses a number of interesting graves including the Adamsons but closed to new burials in 1933. One of the longest funeral processions ever seen here followed a fatality at Heworth Colliery in 1933.

Right: Church interior following the restoration. This little church developed a whole network of various groups. In 1922 the church had a Sunday School, bible classes, Mothers Union, Church Benefit Society, Boy Scouts (Troop no 30 Gateshead) and a children's guild.

Matthew Plummer's worries about the rise of Methodism were well founded. The Methodists first recorded meeting places was in James Stead's house at the Stead. A new Wesleyan Methodist chapel was later opened on 28th March 1833. They then seem to have had fairly sporadic meetings until September 1898 when the chapel was converted to a pair of shops.

Primitive Methodism first seems to have been preached at Windy Nook in 1821 and two years later a camp meeting was held at which it was recorded *'a few got saved'*. On the 8th September 1863, the foundation stone was laid for a new chapel followed by tea at the Mechanics' Institute. The building opened on 2nd April 1864. About 300 attended and they all sat down to an afternoon soiree later. Inside, the building contained a chapel and a small schoolroom with a vestry. The total bill for the chapel was £350 but as £200 was collected on the opening day, they were soon well on the way to clearing the debt. The Sunday School grew and by 1898 there were 30 teachers and 70 scholars. In 1906, the foundation stone for a new hall was laid.

Windy Nook also had members of the Methodist New Connexion. By 1844, 15 members were recorded here. They first met at a cottage (*seen right*) on Stone Street that was later occupied by Philip and Catherine Stephenson.

Right: Philip Stephenson, outside his house, number 2 Stone Street.

A new chapel was opened on 13th June 1865 on Albion Street. This was the Ebenezer Chapel, built by stone from Kell's quarries by Thomas Kay (of Kay's Buildings). The stone cost £420 and Kay charged £55 to build it. Within twenty years, the chapel was in financial difficulties and it seemed that it would have to close. However, such was the strength of support for the chapel that members mortgaged their own homes to save it.

The chapel was extended in 1903 to accommodate the growing Sunday School and to add a vestry. One hundred and twenty yards of land was bought for £25 1s 6d and Wilkinson, a Felling builder, did the work. In 1904, the Sunday School was recorded as having 16 teachers and 98 scholars. Finally in 1910, the Society's last debt was paid off and a service of thanksgiving was held on 6th October.

Music was always important and singing was a regular feature. A temperance band began in the 1860s and while they may not all have been members of the chapel, they used it for band practice. The Northern Regional Brass Band competition was held in the chapel in 1874. The chapel choir always went out carol singing at Christmas. One of the most prominent members was John Patterson, a trustee and a devout Sunday School worker, who was murdered at the Co-op in 1907.

Following the Act of Methodist Union, there was a major overhaul of the circuits in 1935. It was then decided to amalgamate the New Connexion Chapel on Stone Street with the Primitive Methodist Chapel on Albion Street. Stone Street was used for worship and Albion Street for youth work.

Left: Ebenezer Chapel members outside the chapel, c. 1925. In 1924, the singing was recorded as being *'of a most helpful character.'*

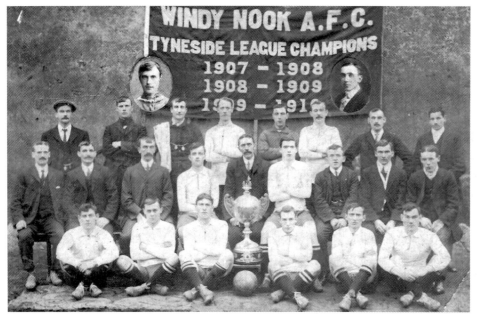

Left: The Windy Nook 'Nobblers'. Windy Nook's ace football team 'the Nobblers' had their glory days in the first decade of the 20th century when they won the Tyneside League four years in succession. They were even filmed in action – the Imperial Cinema at Felling showed a short film of a match between the Nobblers and Felling E.R. (Equal Rights) Club in February 1911.

Right: Of course no mention of Windy Nook would be complete without mention of its windmill, which, although referred to on maps as Heworth windmill, was certainly not in Heworth! Situated on the Causeway, this was a three floored stone building which was also known as Blue Quarries mill or Snowdon's mill, after the three brothers who built it in the 18th century. It was originally about 70 feet high and was one of many damaged during the famous

'windy Monday' storm of 1839. It was last worked in 1879 and demolished in 1964. There was however, once another mill in Windy Nook which was actually called Windy Nook mill and this was situated behind the present day Albion Street and Stone Street.

Left: The first school in Windy Nook appears to have been that run by John 'Cooky' Henderson in Stone Street during the 1820s which was known as Henderson's Academy. In 1836, Matthew Plummer, the Vicar of Heworth, established a school in two cottages near the top of the Stead. A new St Alban's Parochial School was built at the top of Coldwell lane in 1843 opposite the Black House. This cost £280 and had a ground floor classroom with a room for the schoolmaster above. Then, in 1870 a new National School opened at High Heworth which served the village successfully until the opening of the much bigger Board School in Albion Street in 1883. After that, attendances declined and the school nearly closed. However, it served until the early 20th century doing double duty as a Mechanics' Institute and then as a church mission hall in the 1920s and 1930s. The school was finally demolished in the 1950s.

The new board school opened under the auspices of the Heworth School Board on 7th May 1883 at a cost of £5,900. It could house 250 infants and 350 juniors and was enlarged in 1892-3. Fifty two children were admitted in the first week who all paid one penny to attend each week.

Right: Windy Nook Board School. The school was built of local sandstone from Kells quarries on land sold by the Church Commissioners for £300. Once opened, it not only replaced the National School at Windy Nook mentioned on the previous page but also the National School at Heworth both of which had been given poor reports by HM Inspectors. The little St Alban's School was dubbed *'inefficient and uncomfortable'* by the Inspectors in 1880 and it was eventually closed and sold with the money made from the sale going towards paying for St Oswald's Mission Church in 1906 which was opened by one of the Adamson daughters.

During a school inspection in 1911 it was remarked that: *'This school is ably supervised, the teaching is energetic, methodical and intelligent and creditable progress is being made.'*

However, it was also remarked that *'During the lessons in writing and kindred subjects, the teachers should take care to see that the children do not stoop too much over the exercises.'*

Left: Windy Nook school children, c. 1900.

Evening classes were also carried on at the school aimed at those entering the local collieries.

In 1915, the infants collected fruit, flowers, eggs, chocolates, cigarettes and socks for patients at Whinney House Hospital in Low Fell.

Right: Windy Nook School football team, 1929-30 season.

Left: Windy Nook School, 1930. The teacher is thought to be William Taylor. The school had its own gardening sheds. During the Second World War, children were encouraged to grow vegetables in the school gardens as part of the 'Dig for Victory' campaign. The school closed for two days in March 1941 due to air raids although no damage was caused to either the school or the area.

Right: Miss Wright's class, 1957. Back row: P. Simon?, R. McManners?, J. Johnson, unknown, unknown, R. Heatherington. Front row: unknown, Owen Parry, unknown, unknown, Neil Anderson and John Wilson.

Because of its healthy situation, Windy Nook was an obvious place to have a fever hospital although this was situated outside the main village. The hospital was essential to the area as outbreaks of infectious diseases were common. In 1914/1915 there were 225 cases of scarlet fever treated here of which 14 died. During severe outbreaks of infectious diseases, nurses from the training homes were used to supplement the regular staff.

By 1912, it was employing a nurse-matron, one charge nurse, one trained nurse, one ward maid and one cook general. The ward maid earned £18 per year plus board, lodging and washing. By 1936 it contained 28 beds and six cots. There were four large wards together with an observation ward with a nurse-matron in charge and a staff of nurses. However, as social conditions improved, admissions became fewer and the hospital closed after the Second World War.

… And finally. Here's a fun image to complete these glimpses of Heworth, Felling and Windy Nook – three areas with interesting histories.

Left: Windy Nook New Connexion concert party, 1920. For some reason, the ladies seem to be dressed as birds.